19.95

D1443765

NO WAY!

WEiRD JOBS

Michael J. Rosen

and Ben Kassoy

Illustrations by Pat Sandy

M Millbrook Press • Minneapolis

Millbrook Press
A division of Lerner Publishing Group, Inc.
241 First Avenue North
Minneapolis, MN 55401 U.S.A.

Website address: www.lernerbooks.com

Main body text set in Adrianna Regular 12/16
Typeface provided by Chank

Rosen, Michael J., 1954–
    Weird jobs / by Michael J. Rosen and Ben Kassoy ; illustrated by Pat
Sandy.
        pages   cm. — (No way!)
    Includes index.
    ISBN 978-0-7613-8983-5 (lib. bdg. : alk. paper)
    ISBN 978-1-4677-1709-0 (eBook)
    1. Occupations—Juvenile literature. I. Kassoy, Ben. II. Sandy, Pat,
illustrator. III. Title.
HF5381.2.R665 2014
331.702—dc23   2012042374

Manufactured in the United States of America
1 – BP – 7/15/13

The authors would like to
recognize the generous
contribution of Christoffer
Strömstedt, as well as the
efforts of Ashley Heestand,
Colin Stoecker, and Claire
Hamilton in the researching,
fact-checking, and drafting
of the No Way! series
of books.

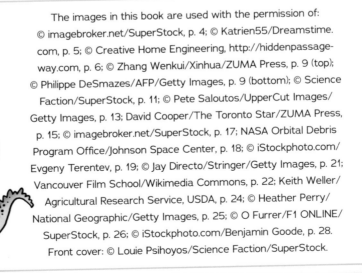

TABLE of CONTENTS

ARCTIC ARCHITECT
ICE HOTEL BUILDER

Any kid can build a snowman. But only an expert can build an entire hotel out of ice. Make that an ex-*brrr*-t!

At Icehotel, tourists can see amazing architecture *and* their own frosty breaths. The hotel stands in Sweden, north of the Arctic Circle. If Santa Claus took vacations, this is where he'd relax after lugging presents around. But for the architects who build Icehotel each year, the project is no holiday.

Huge steel beams form the outside of the hotel. Special machines spray ice onto these beams. (Picture a snowblower crossed with a blowtorch.) Once the coating freezes, builders remove the metal frame. All that remain are the wintry walls and the icy ceiling.

Visitors to Sweden's Icehotel prepare for a frosty stroll.

Next, builders have to figure out how to create hallways, a lobby, and guest rooms out of ice blocks. A team of designers shapes every other icy item in the hotel's interior. That means ice tables, ice chairs, ice glasses, and even icicle silverware. (It also means that guests wear winter gloves both indoors and out!)

Alas, the job only lasts six weeks. Come springtime, this winter wonderland turns into a hotel-sized puddle.

HiDE AND SECRET
SECRET PASSAGEWAY DESIGNER

Most spies, detectives, and superheroes have a trapdoor or hidden passage somewhere in their hideout. Any good movie or comic book will tell you that. Thanks to secret passageway designers, these hidden spaces are moving from the big screen into your living room. Designers are skilled builders. They're gifted with electronics too. Not to mention sneakiness!

Designers meet with clients to discuss the disguised spaces. Should a painting pop out of its frame and reveal a safe? Should a staircase lift up and lead to a playroom? Each project requires lots of planning. And whispering.

A designer creates a computer model of a passageway before building the life-sized version. This helps the designer predict how everything will fit together.

Every secret passage needs a secret way to get inside. Magnets, remote controls, and radio signals are all ways to unlock a tricky trigger. Tipping a dictionary could open a room behind a bookcase. Lifting the right chess piece could reveal a trapdoor.

If you have somewhere between $5,000 and $50,000 in your piggy bank, you could have your own hideaway. Disappear from parents, siblings, and chores! Just beware of nosey neighbors when your designer's installing the secret passage.

People often ask pro designers how many sneaky nooks they have in their own houses. For most, the answer is zero! With all the requests from *other* people, these designers hardly have time to sneak away for a nap.

HAVE A BLAST
DEMOLITION BLASTER

"Everybody loves blowing stuff up," says Cody Gustafson.

Duh! But some people love it more than others. Take professional demolitionists like Gustafson. They get *paid* to smash things. In Cody's world, *ka-boom* equals *cha-ching!*

People hire these master blasters to destroy all sorts of things. Bridges, shopping malls, skyscrapers. Each structure comes crashing downward so that something new can be built from the ground up.

Sound like a kid's dream job? Sorry, demolition is not child's play. Even expert blasters need a license!

Blasters look closely at the landmark they're going to topple. They pick explosives to match the building's shape, its location, and the materials from which it was made. Buildings are like snowflakes. No two are alike.

A 3-D computer model helps blasters choose where to load each explosive. Most are placed at the bottom of the building. The placement of each one directs the way the building falls. Once blasters have double-checked the setup for safety, they attach a trigger to the explosives. Then, with a press of the button . . . *boom!*

As the dust settles, dump trucks arrive to pick up the pieces. The blasters move on. Their next target? Well, what goes up must come down. So there's no shortage of work for a demolitionist.

IT'S THE PiTS!
ODOR TESTER

Bad breath, body odor, wet sneakers, rotten food—and let's not even open the bathroom door. We live amid stink. But imagine the *pee-yew!* of the world if we had no forces to fight the funk! Thank goodness for air fresheners, mouthwash, and deodorant. And thanks to the nosey professionals who test them.

Odor raters make sure that stench-fighting products work. They get to inhale the fumes of a reeking room before and after a blast of air freshener. Mouthwash testers get up close and personal with bad breath. Deodorant testers sniff sweaty pits. No pinched nostrils or gas masks are allowed on these jobs!

A trio of breath testers gets a whiff of what some volunteers had for lunch.

One perfectly pleasant person spends all day rating odors from the *other* end. Michael Levitt is a stomach and intestine doctor. He studies flatulence (farts) to sniff out health problems.

Levitt has captured more than one thousand smelly samples. His job is a game of smell and tell. He takes a whiff of each little jar and reviews the results. So what does his nose note as the nastiest smell? The "rotten egg" scent of hydrogen sulfide.

You find these findings foolish? Stink again! "The odors of feces [poop] and intestinal gas could be important markers of [stomach] health," Levitt says. Levitt notes that too much hydrogen sulfide in a toot can indicate a life-threatening disease.

That's right: Levitt is finding out what kinds of farts are truly silent but deadly.

BODY OF WORK
LiVE-BRAiN ARTiST

Drawing a realistic portrait isn't easy. It's tough to capture the details of a face and the folds of clothing.

Now imagine drawing a portrait of a person's insides. But you're in an operating room instead of a studio. Surgeons are crowding around your subject. Lights flash! Blood splatters! Someone's life is at stake!

Sounds impossible, right? Well, if you're like medical illustrator Neil Hardy, then drawing a kidney is a piece of cake!

Hardy's specialty is portraits of people's innards. He started out as a doctor. But for the last fifty years, he has hovered *behind* surgeons. He has often sketched the human brain. As a doctor slices and dices, Hardy etches and sketches. This job has many challenges, but asking his subjects to sit still isn't one of them. They're knocked out cold!

As the surgeon's scalpel draws blood, so Hardy draws what's under the skin! His drawings have appeared in many textbooks, journals, and films. Medical students study his drawings before they face the real thing. Quite the *body* of work!

Hardy can do things even advanced cameras can't. He can remove details that interfere with what's important to see. He can show all the stages of a process on a single page. He can highlight what's important in an image with clear outlines or different colors.

A fair share of would-be doctors faint while watching surgery. But there's no time for a queasy stomach when you're hired to draw one!

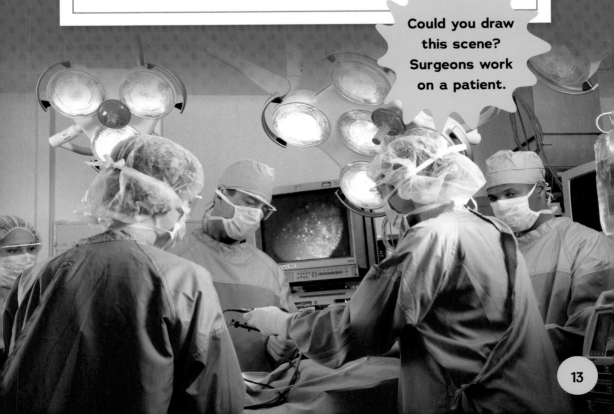

Could you draw this scene? Surgeons work on a patient.

BEST WITH BEASTS
ANIMAL TRAINER

Most pet tricks aren't all that tricky to teach. But only the best can train rodents to play sports, dogs to find bedbugs, or birds to protect runways.

STAR RATS

Dr. Alliston Reid is half psychology professor, half basketball coach. He teaches teams of rats to scurry down a mini court. They even dunk a mini ball into a mini hoop!

Coaching these small feet is no small feat. Reid's training secret? Positive reinforcement. That means he rewards correct actions. When a rat makes a basket, it earns a rat treat. Go, team!

PEST-CONTROL POOCH

Dogs can learn to sniff out nearly anything. All they need is practice, that same positive reinforcement, and some doggie treats. Some dogs search for criminals. Some seek out skiers buried in snow. And some dogs even hunt for tiny bedbugs!

No one sleeps tight when bedbugs bite. But in fifteen minutes, a dog can find 96 percent of them. Then pest control can focus on getting rid of these little nightmares.

FLIGHT CONTROL

There's plenty of room in the sky. But around an airport, the air is only big enough for one bird: the giant metal kind. Oh, and a few falcons.

An airspace falcon trainer's raptors chase other birds from the airspace. Raptors are among the fastest flying birds. They also shoo hogs or deer from the runway. Such animals could interfere with a pilot's takeoffs and landings. But thanks to falcon trainers, it's hello safety, bye-bye birdies!

FORE! SCORE!
GOLF BALL RETRIEVER

In golf, you can drive, putt, chip, or slice your ball. Just try not to soak it. The last place you want a ball to land is underwater. That is, unless you're a professional golf ball retriever.

What's bad news for golfers can be good news for gophers. You know, the people who *go for* the balls.

Wearing a wet suit and breathing gear, a diver wades into a pond or a lake with a giant sack. He or she slogs through muck and grime. Then the diver plunges to the bottom to scrounge up lost balls. Sometimes, the water is so murky a diver can hardly see. He or she has to feel around blindly for the balls. Sometimes divers even pick up balls with their feet.

Plunges into golf course ponds can be hazardous. Divers often come face-to-face with snapping turtles, snakes, or even alligators. So what do you do if a gator tries to steal your bag of golf balls? "Go for the eyes," one retriever says. And you thought golf was *boring?*

Why do divers risk danger to reclaim lost balls? Turns out they are sunken treasures. A diver can bag up to twenty thousand balls in a day. Every ball is washed, sorted, and resold. Even if each ball is only worth a few cents, well, do the math! They could be worth $400!

So swing away, bad golfers. One person's *fore!* is another person's *score!*

DEFENDER OF THE PLANET!
ORBITAL DEBRIS SCIENTIST

This illustration shows the dangerous debris within 1,243 miles (2,000 kilometers) of Earth.

Half a million pieces of space trash orbit planet Earth. These objects whiz around at something like 20,000 miles (32,187 km) per hour. That could spell bad news for earthlings. Let's say some speeding trash hits a spacecraft or a satellite. *Smash!* If only the twinkling stars in the sky were stoplights.

Thankfully, orbital debris scientist Nick Johnson is here to defend the planet.

"Spacecraft are always throwing things off," Johnson explains. An orbiting object as tiny as a paint chip can break a spaceship window. A lost screw could poke a hole in a satellite! Worse, each crash can chip off yet more debris.

Johnson is part of a team at the National Aeronautics and Space Administration (NASA). The NASA team tracks the position and movement of space waste. It uses math to figure out when crashes might happen. When the chance is greater than one in ten thousand, the team works to get the debris out of the way.

If a spacecraft is in danger, Johnson orders the astronauts to change the flight path. But sometimes Earth itself is at risk. In 2006, a busted satellite was barreling toward our home planet! Johnson gave advice to the U.S. president himself. "We struck it with a missile," Johnson says. "Eliminated the threat."

And you were worried about an alien invasion? *Please!*

IN THE SWIM
PROFESSIONAL MERMAID

You say you want to earn your living underwater? Exactly what sort of job do you imagine? Whatever you're thinking, chances are professional mermaid didn't come to mind. But that's just what Linden Wolbert is. Her workplace is the deep-blue sea.

If you're ever in the Philippines, wave hello to this trio of pro mermaids.

Wolbert started out as a swimmer, diving instructor, and world-class free diver. (*Free diving* means "swimming as far below the surface as possible—in one breath!") Her friends began calling her Mermaid. She took that name to heart. Linden hired a designer to create a 35-pound (16-kilogram) tail that she could wear while swimming. It works the way a real mermaid's tail would work. She can push herself through the water by kicking the tail fin. And get this: having an 8-foot (2.4-meter) tail means sharks are afraid of *her!*

Wolbert's skills launched her job as an underwater model. Not everyone can hold his or her breath for more than five minutes. (Maybe she *is* part fish after all!) Then she became a full-time "edu-tainer." She gives talks about clean oceans and water-safety skills. Of course, she comes to the surface before speaking. It's hard to understand a stream of bubbles!

SOUNDS LiKE FUN!
FOLEY ARTiST

Foley artists can make the *thunk* of a bowling ball into the *smack* of a superhero fight scene.

When someone says the words *movie magic*, you probably think of the explosions or fake aliens you see on-screen. But you *hear* magic at the movies too.

Let's say you're viewing a superhero battle. You hear a big *smack!* and then the bad guy falls down. But that smacking sound? It didn't happen on the movie set.

When a film is shot, some sounds are too quiet for a microphone to pick up. Some are so loud that they would drown out the actors' voices. So people called Foley artists re-create or tweak almost every sound you hear.

First, Foley artists view a filmed scene on a large screen. Then they match a new sound to where it would occur during the scene.

This odd occupation is named for Jack Foley. He was a Hollywood sound worker in the 1930s. He invented many of the tricks that re-create hums, crashes, creaks, and splashes within films.

For Foley artists, some sounds are a snap. If a bride is running in high heels, they'll rap two shoes against the ground.

Other noises demand creativity. Need a horse's gallop? Hit two coconuts together! A skier carving through snow? Whack at a bag of breakfast cereal and cornstarch.

So what was the sound of that superhero punch? Celery stalks wrapped in a wet sponge, smacked against a foam mat. The next time you're watching a movie, see if you can guess what's making the sounds that lead to movie magic.

DOO-DOO DUTY
MANURE INSPECTOR

Smell that? Scientist Terry Whitehead collects pig manure to test for bacteria.

Are you a maniac in the mud? Dude of the dirt? Girl gone gritty? Maybe you're the messiest kid on the playground! But would you care to spend your career in piles of poop?

Thankfully, some people do just that. Manure inspectors such as Michael Doyle keep us safe and keep food yummy in our tummies.

Every year, cattle produce more than 1 billion tons (0.9 billion metric tons) of manure. Farmers use this manure to fertilize their fields. That's right: our veggies grow in doo-doo. The method may sound nasty, but it's not as nasty as the germs sometimes found in manure.

If an animal carries harmful bacteria, its poop does as well. So will any foods that grow in the fields fertilized with that manure. Eating this food can make humans seriously sick. So Doyle works to keep the manure clean. Knee-deep in doo-doo, he makes sure that harmful germs don't get into our fruits and veggies. (Seriously, spinach doesn't need to be any harder to swallow.)

"We have to wade through a lot of poop," Doyle says. "Even when you wear gloves, the [poop] smell tends to get [stuck] in your skin."

All the ickiness pays off. Doyle and his team have stopped a harmful type of bacteria called *E. coli* from invading all kinds of foods. He created a wash that kills the bacteria without harming the food itself. His recipe won him a big award! And no, it wasn't Smelliest Scientist of the Year.

IT'S A BIRD!
IT'S A PLANE! IT'S A...
SKYDIVING INSTRUCTOR

Dan Brodsky-Chenfeld may not be a superhero, but he flies like one. He's a professional skydiver and skydiving instructor.

Check out these numbers. He has fallen from 12,000 feet (3,658 m) more than twenty-three thousand times at more than 120 miles (193 km) per hour.

Brodsky-Chenfeld began falling from the skies as a five-year-old. He started by jumping off his bunk bed. Turns out a pillowcase is not an effective parachute. But bumps and bruises couldn't keep him down. He's just gone up, up, up!

Brodsky-Chenfeld first jumped from a plane while in college. By that time, there were no parents nearby to put him in time-out! Still, he wanted his mommy once he started to fall. "I've never been so terrified," he admits.

Since that first jump, he has become one of the world's most famous skydivers. He's won seven skydiving world championships and nineteen national championships. These days, his trophies outnumber any bumps and bruises.

Brodsky-Chenfeld is so high above the rest that he trains the world's top divers. In formation skydiving competitions, teams create unique shapes as they fall. Just picture snowflakes made of spinning humans. Brodsky-Chenfeld coaches these athletes with practices, weight lifting, and even meditation. In 2002, he designed a three-hundred-skydiver jump from fourteen different planes. That set a free-fall world record. Next, he's planning a jump in the emirate of Dubai, in the Middle East, for five hundred skydivers from all over the world. Talk about taking a sport to new heights!

FiDDLiNG AROUND

EXPERiMENTAL MUSiCiAN

Great musicians master their instruments. They work hard to create great music. But amazing musicians *create* their instruments. They make music the world has never heard before.

Jon Rose began playing violin as a child. But at age fifteen, he'd had enough of formal training. He didn't bow out of music, though. Instead, he started making his own bows—and violins too!

Imagine playing music with a barbed-wire fence!

To see a *real* bicycle-powered instrument, check out http://www.jonroseweb.com!

These instruments aren't your average violins. Rose calls them "relative violins." They may sound impossible to play, but they're the real deal! Take Rose's bicycle-powered double violin. To make this instrument, he attached two violins to the wheel of a bicycle. The violins play when the wheel is spun. What happens if the wheel turns backward? You guessed it. The sound rewinds itself!

Rose has rigged violins to radios, windmills, and even boats. He has also played an entire concert with only chain saws. The sharp sounds made the audience want to cut a rug!

Rose has also completed twelve-hour marathon performances. He even once played barbed-wire fences in the Australian outback, using a violin as the bow. *Wow!* Err, *ow!* Sometimes Rose realizes a project is "HUP: Hopeless, useless, pointless." But he keeps at it. After all, the show must go on.

GLOSSARY

architect: a person who designs buildings, spaces, or communities

Arctic Circle: an imaginary line that marks off the Arctic, the northernmost area of the planet

bacteria: simple, one-celled creatures that may live in other creatures, sometimes causing them harm

bow: a curved stick strung with fibers. A bow moves against the strings of an instrument to create sound.

cut a rug: dance

debris: small parts of something that has been shattered or broken

demolitionist: a person whose job is to destroy things such as buildings and bridges

experimental: attempting something that has not been tested or may not work as planned

feat: a difficult achievement

fertilize: to add nutrients that help plants to grow

fore: a word that golfers shout to warn people about flying golf balls

hydrogen sulfide: a chemical compound that can poison the human body in high levels

license: proof of someone's permission to own something or to perform some specific task

manure: poop from animals that is used to help plants grow

medical: related to the treatment of disease or injury, or the science of human well-being

meditation: focusing thoughts for a long period of time. This is practiced for religious reasons or for relaxation.

orbit: to circle an object

raptor: a bird that hunts its prey, such as a hawk, a falcon, or an owl

relative: similar to something else because it has one or more qualities in common

robotics: the designing and building of robots

satellite: an object that orbits the moon or another larger body in outer space

wet suit: a tight waterproof suit that keeps swimmers and divers warm in cold water

SOURCE NOTES

8   Cody Gustafson, quoted in "Demolition Blaster," *PopularMechanics.com*, February 11, 2010, http://www.popularmechanics.com/outdoors/extreme-jobs/4345650 (July 30, 2012).

17   "Dirty Jobs: Golfball Diver," *Discovery.com*, http://dsc.discovery.com/tv-shows/dirty-jobs/videos /golfball-diver.htm (July 30, 2012).

18   Nick Johnson, quoted in "Clearing Some Space," *University of Memphis Magazine*, 2009, http://www.memphis.edu/magazine/issues/summer09/space.php (July 30, 2012).

19   Ibid.

25   Michael Doyle, quoted in "The Worst Jobs in Science," *PopSci*, January 26, 2009, http://www.popsci.com /scitech/gallery/2009-01/worst-jobs-science?image=46 (July 30, 2012).

27   "TedxFlanders – Dan Brodsky-Chenfeld," YouTube video, posted by TedxTales, October 4, 2011 http://www. youtu.be/MHEMVhNEluI (July 30, 2012).

29   "The Relative Violins," *The Jon Rose Web*, 2001, http://www.jonroseweb.com/d_picts_relviolins_describe .html (July 30, 2012).

FURTHER READING

BOOKS

Loy, Jessica. *When I Grow Up: A Young Person's Guide to Interesting and Unusual Occupations.* New York: Henry Holt, 2008.
Want the inside scoop on being an alpaca farmer? What about a chocolate maker or a lobsterman? Those jobs are among the fourteen unusual careers featured in this book.

Marisco, Katie. *Stinky Sanitation Inventions.* Minneapolis: Lerner Publications, 2014.
If you liked learning about odor testers, pick up this book to meet the people behind many smelly inventions.

Schiff, Nancy Rica. *Odder Jobs: More Portraits of Unusual Occupations.* Berkeley, CA: Ten Speed Press, 2006. This book features black-and-white photographs of even more peculiar occupations.

Weiss, Ellen. *Odd Jobs: The Wackiest Jobs You've Never Heard Of.* New York: Aladdin, 2012.
This photo-packed book takes a look at twelve other interesting careers including roller coaster designer, food stylist, and storm chaser.

WEBSİTES

Kids.Gov: Jobs
http://kids.usa.gov/jobs/index .shtml
Check out this site to learn more about the job that might be best for you someday. Find out what it's like to be a chef, an FBI agent, or one of many other occupations.

U.S. Bureau of Labor Statistics: A–Z List of Careers
http://www.bls.gov/k12/azlist .htm
The Bureau of Labor Statistics has an A–Z listing of dozens of jobs, complete with kid-friendly explanations. Each entry explains the job's responsibilities, the training and preparation needed, the pay, and a few other aspects.

INDEX